PERSONALIZED PERFUMES

PERSONALIZED PERFUMES

More than 40 recipes
for making fragrances
with essential oils

More than 40 recipes

for making fragrances

with essential oils

GAIL DUFF

SIMON &
SCHUSTER

NEW YORK LONDON TORONTO SYDNEY TOKYO SINGAPORE

SIMON & SCHUSTER
Simon & Schuster Building
Rockefeller Center
1230 Avenue of the Americas
New York, New York 10020

Conceived and produced by Breslich & Foss, London

Designed by Roger Daniels

Printed in Italy

10 9 8 7 6 5 4 3 2 1

Library of Congress Cataloging-in-Publication Data
Duff, Gail
    Personalized perfumes: more than 40 recipes for making perfumes with
essential oils / by Gail Duff
        p. cm.
        ISBN 0–671–88029–2
        1. Perfume–Amateur's manuals. I. Title.
TP983.D84 1994
668'.542–dc20

93–31704
CIP

ACKNOWLEDGMENTS
The extract from *Dedicatory Ode* by Hilaire Belloc on page 47 is
reprinted by permission of the Peters Fraser & Dunlop Group Ltd.

The extract from *Cargoes* by John Masefield on page 64 is reprinted
by permission of the Society of Authors as the literary representative
of the Estate of John Masefield.

Every effort has been made to trace the copyright holders of the quoted material.
If, however, there are any omissions, these can be rectified in future editions.

Author's Note: To the best of my knowledge, there are no commercially
manufactured perfumes marketed under any of the names given to perfumes in
this book. If, however, names have been inadvertently duplicated, the perfume
bearing the name is not intended in any way to be a replica of the manufactured
product.

Some of the oils mentioned in this book can cause allergic reactions. It is always
advisable to carry out a patch test before applying oils liberally to your skin.

Contents

Introduction

Were not summer's distillations left
A liquid prisoner, pent in walls of glass,
Beauty's effect of beauty was bereft,
Nor it, nor no remembrance what it was;
But flowers distilled, though they with winter meet,
Leese but their show, their substance still lives sweet.

WILLIAM SHAKESPEARE

A sensory signature, an extension of your personality, an aura that gives you glamour and mystery, and makes you feel utterly feminine — perfume is all of these. A final dab of scent complements your outfit, increases your confidence, and sets you up for the evening: you'd feel undressed without it. But as well as giving immense personal pleasure, perfume can also relax you, revive you, enhance a good mood, chase away a bad one, pep you up — or help you go to sleep. It's a lot more than just a nice smell.

ESSENTIAL OILS

Most scents are made by mixing the essential oils of plants, each oil having its own particular fragrance and effect.

There are numerous oils and countless combinations to suit all moods and tastes.

Every plant contains essential oil, which can be described as being the "life force" of the plant. Not only does the oil contain the true scent of the plant, it also contains the natural — and often theraputic — properties of that plant. Some are relaxing, some uplifting, and some are reputed to have aphrodisiac qualities. The skill in making up a perfume lies in creating a blend that not only smells the way you want, but also acts in the way you want.

For thousands of years, essential oils have been in use as medicines, perfumes, and cosmetics, as well as ingredients in cookery and religious rituals. The original method of obtaining the essential oil from a plant was to soak the flowers or leaves in oil or melted fat, so that the plant's scent gradually dissolved into it. It was a long, tedious process. In the tenth century A.D., an Arabian doctor called Avicenna discovered the secret of distilling, and by the sixteenth century most large country houses in Europe had a "stillroom," or distillery. Although this was mainly used for making alcoholic drinks, the lady of the house and her maids also used the apparatus for extracting the oils from different flowers in the garden. They made perfumes, toilet waters, and other potions for keeping both face and body beautiful. When you are making your own perfumes today, there is no need to begin at the very beginning. Producing an essential oil at home by macerating flowers in olive oil, for example,

is never very successful, and to own a still is now illegal! Essential oils are produced commercially, either by distillation or by expression (pressing). The results are excellent and often economical. There has never been a better time than the present for buying a wide range of good quality oils at reasonable prices.

Buying Essential Oils

Plants contain varying amounts of oil, and this is the main factor determining the availability and price of the different oils. The citrus fruits — orange, lime, and lemon — all have skins that are covered in tiny pockets of oil that you can see and smell when you peel them. At the other extreme, it takes around one ton of rose petals to produce 11oz of rose oil. Somewhere in the middle are the herbal oils, such as rosemary and coriander. These have strong scents and produce relatively large amounts of oil.

In order to create your own perfumes from essential oils, you will need to build up a selection gradually. Buying every single oil in this book at once would be very expensive and you might find that some of them are barely used. This book is divided into sections, according to the emotions and personality traits that the perfumes are intended to suit. You may like to choose oils from one particular section, or to buy those that are the most popular overall. To help you choose, here are the numbers of times that the oils are used in each section and throughout the book as a whole.

ESSENTIAL OIL	USED THROUGHOUT BOOK	CONFIDENCE	RELAXATION	VITALITY	HAPPINESS	LOVE AND LUXURY
BASIL	3	1	1	1	0	0
BERGAMOT	9	3	1	1	4	0
CARNATION	2	0	0	1	1	0
CEDARWOOD	2	1	0	1	0	0
CINNAMON	4	1	0	1	2	0
CLARY SAGE	3	0	0	2	1	0
CLOVE	3	0	1	2	0	0
CORIANDER	3	2	0	0	0	1
CYPRESS	2	1	0	0	0	1
FRANKINCENSE	1	0	1	0	0	0
GARDENIA	2	0	0	0	0	2
GINGER	1	0	0	0	0	1
GRAPEFRUIT	6	3	0	1	2	0
JASMINE	13	2	1	3	5	2
JUNIPER	1	0	0	0	1	0
LAVENDER	4	1	1	2	0	0
LEMON	8	2	1	3	2	0
LEMON VERBENA	2	0	1	1	0	0
LIME	5	1	1	1	1	1
LINDEN-BLOSSOM	1	0	0	0	0	1
MANDARIN	3	0	0	2	1	0
MUSK	2	0	1	0	0	1
NEROLI	8	2	2	0	1	3
OAKMOSS	4	2	0	0	0	2
ORANGE	7	0	2	1	1	3
PATCHOULI	3	1	0	0	1	1
PINE	1	0	1	0	0	0
ROSE	8	1	2	1	3	1
ROSE GERANIUM	1	0	0	0	0	1
ROSEWOOD	2	1	0	0	0	1
SANDALWOOD	14	1	3	2	3	5
SPEARMINT	3	0	1	0	1	1
SWEET ORANGE	1	1	0	0	0	0
VANILLA	2	0	1	0	0	1
VIOLET	1	1	0	0	0	0
YLANG YLANG	6	3	1	2	0	0

Natural and Synthetic Oils

As has already been said, some plants yield only minute amounts of oil, and others yield relatively large amounts. Obviously, the natural oils that are more copiously produced are going to be the least expensive and most readily available.

The most expensive oils are the delicate flower oils, namely rose, jasmine, and neroli. Their prices also fluctuate, so much so that most catalogues list "price on request." A quick look at the chart above will tell you that these are among the most used oils in this book, and this is probably true of almost any collection of perfume recipes. To satisfy this demand, synthetic oils have been produced and are available much more cheaply. So which should you buy?

If you intend to use the oils for aromatherapy, you need to buy the real thing. Synthetic oils smell good, but otherwise have no theraputic effect. If you are making up perfumes for fun, then the synthetic oils are quite satisfactory, certainly for your first experiments as a *perfumier*. You may, later on, become so interested in oils and their effects that you will start to buy the real thing. Oils are only used by the drop, and you'll find that a little goes a very long way. Certain flower oils are only available in their synthetic form. Those used in this book are gardenia, carnation, and violet. These, along with musk oil (which is always synthetically produced today) cannot be used in aromatherapy.

Buying and Storing Oils

Oils are becoming more readily available as interest in their therapeutic effect grows. Always buy them labelled, from reputable suppliers. Some mail order oils come in small, dark-colored bottles that are fitted with dropper tops or plastic inserts under the screw caps that enable you to measure them out by the drop.

Store oils in a cool, dark place. They have a shelf-life of about two years. Do make sure that they are safely shut away from children and animals, as, although some oils can be used in cooking, others are toxic. If any oil has been swallowed, it is best not to try to induce vomiting, but to seek urgent medical help. If the oils come into contact with your eyes, rinse them thoroughly with cold water.

BLENDING PERFUMES

When it comes to perfume, likes and dislikes vary tremendously; perfumes also smell different on different people. Obviously, people have their own preferences, but these can also vary according to mood — you may adore a perfume one day, and be quite indifferent to it the next. This is because different oils can trigger or enhance particular emotions. One day you may feel happy and carefree, the next you may feel as if your batteries are a little low, and you need to withdraw into yourself to re-charge them. The scents that you use need to reflect changes of mood.

In the nineteenth century, a Frenchman called Piesse revolutionized perfumery by working out a way of classifying scents. It was very similar to music, with "top notes," "middle notes," and "base notes." Top notes, such as the citrus scents or less intense herbs such as basil, are fresh and light. When you smell a perfume, the top notes are the scents you smell first. However, they soon evaporate, revealing the middle notes, which are the scents that form the true "character" of the blend. The middle notes consist of most of the floral oils, some of the herbals, and one or two of the lighter woods and spices, such as geranium, lavender, clove, and coriander. The base notes are richer, heavier, warming scents — usually the woods, spices, and resins. They also include rose and jasmine. Ideally, a perfume should contain top, middle, and base notes.

Ingredients

To make a perfume for yourself, you will need a selection of essential oils, plus a base which will act as a carrier. Alcohol or oils of various kinds can be used as this base. When you are experimenting with mixtures of scents that you have never used before, do not use a base that is either too complicated or too expensive. Use one of the cheaper, good quality, unscented oils such as wheatgerm, avocado, or almond. These are fine for discovering and perfecting the right blend of essential oils and can often be bought from the same place as you buy your essential oils. However, they do have a very rich, oily quality which can sometimes come through the perfumed oils. They also tend to coat the skin with oil, rather than being absorbed into it.

The best oil to use as a base is jojoba oil. It is more expensive than the others, and therefore best used only when all your experiments are done. Jojoba is not technically an oil but is a liquid wax. It never becomes rancid, so perfumes made with it have a long shelf life. When put onto the skin it soon dries, leaving only the fragrance behind.

Using alcohol as a base gives a fresher, less rich effect to the perfumes. It is best to use a scentless, odorless spirit, such as vodka. Use it mixed half and half with jojoba oil, and always remember that the mixture must be shaken well before use.

For a really inexpensive mixture, you can use vodka mixed with a little glycerin (1½ teaspoons vodka to ½ tea-

spoon glycerin). However, jojoba gives a far better texture and final perfume. All the recipes in this book use 2 teaspoons of base to the drops of oil given.

Equipment

Small pot or container such as an egg-cup

Measuring spoon, or 1 or 2 teaspoons

Dropper (or dropper top from an oil bottle)

Plastic wrap

Perfume funnel or other small funnel

Small dark bottle

Method

1 Measure 2 teaspoons base into your container.

2 Add the essential oils one drop at a time and shake or agitate well after each addition. Test the smell as you go along to make sure you like it.

3 Cover the container with plastic wrap and leave for 12 hours in a cool, dark place for the scents to blend and settle. If the resulting perfume is to your liking, transfer it, using the funnel, to the bottle, and store it in a cool, dark place.

Points to Remember

This book concentrates mainly on using scented oils for fun. The recipes here are devised with the aromatherapy uses of the oils in mind, but they are not cure-alls, and should not be treated as such. Should you become more deeply interested in the beneficial effects of oils, it would help to pay a visit to an aromatherapist or take an aromatherapy course.

As with commercially produced perfume, the various scents in this book will smell different on different skin types. If you don't like the results of your experiments, don't get too disheartened; trying them out is all part of the fun. And remember, you don't have to stick rigidly to the perfume recipes in this book. There are some pages at the end for you to take notes and write down the recipes for your own favorite concoctions — perfumes which really will be unique to you.

Of the oils mentioned in this book, clove and cinnamon may cause skin irritation. If you have sensitive skin, always do a "patch test" before applying the perfume. As a general rule, you should not apply any essential oil *directly* onto your skin.

If you are pregnant, aromatherapists advise against using mixtures that contain the following: basil, clary sage, cedarwood, cypress, juniper, and rose.

Lemon, lime, and bergamot are slightly photosensitive and should not be worn if you plan to sunbathe or lie under a sun lamp.

Layering Scents

When you have found a perfume that you particularly like, you will not want it to clash with other toiletries that you use, such as soap or talcum powder. Using toiletries with similar scents to your main perfume is called "layering" scents. Here are some ways in which you can do this (the ingredients do not include base oil):

COLOGNE
You will need a 5oz bottle for this. Pour in 4fl oz clear vodka, plus double the amount of ingredients given in the chosen perfume recipe. Cover the bottle tightly and shake well. Leave it to mature for at least two days before using.

TOILET WATER
Into your 5oz bottle, pour 2fl oz clear vodka. Add double the amount of ingredients given in the perfume recipe, cover tightly and shake well. Mature for at least two days before using. Shake well before use.

BATH OIL
You will need a base of treated castor oil, pure and odorless, that disperses well in water. To 2fl oz of base oil, add double the amount of ingredients given in the perfume recipe.

Cover the bottle tightly, shake well, and leave for at least a week to mature. Use one tablespoon per bath.

BATH VINEGAR

Add twice the amount of ingredients given in the perfume recipe to 5fl oz of light cider vinegar. Cover the bottle tightly, shake well, and leave for one week. Add 5fl oz of bath vinegar to the bath while the taps are running.

HAND CREAM

Place 6oz petroleum jelly and 4oz beeswax into a saucepan and melt them over a low heat. Stir in half the amount of ingredients given in the perfume recipe. Take the pan away from the heat and let the mixture cool before pouring it into a pot.

CLEANSING CREAM

Place ½ oz beeswax and 1oz lanolin in a double boiler and melt gently over a low heat. Remove from the heat but keep the top part of the double boiler in the water. Using a wooden spoon, slowly add 3fl oz almond oil. Stir in 2 table-spoons spring water (or rose water if you are using a rose perfume), and 2 teaspoons honey. Add half the amount of ingredients given in the perfume recipe. Place the mixture in a container, and store it in a cool place. You can use it just as soon as it is cool.

Talcum Powder

Mix together 3oz unscented talcum powder, 3oz rice flour or cornstarch, ½ tablespoon boric acid powder, and 1 tablespoon crushed orris root powder, plus the amount of oils given in the perfume recipe. Rub the oils in with your fingertips until the mixture feels dry. Sieve the mixture at least twice before using.

Shampoo

Place ½ oz soapwort root in a saucepan with 2½ pints water. Bring it to the boil, cover, and simmer for 4 minutes. Take the pan from the heat, and leave the brew covered until it is quite cool. Strain it, pressing the mixture down well with a spoon. When choosing oils to scent this shampoo, choose the ones that are good for hair, such as lemon and clary sage (rosemary and chamomile oil are also good for hair). Try your blends out on blotting paper first. Then add 2 teaspoons of oil to the shampoo, bottle it, cover tightly, and leave for one week.

To use the shampoo, wet your hair, and pour 7fl oz of the shampoo over it. Rub it in as you would an ordinary shampoo.

Soap

Buy a cake of unscented soap. Soak cotton balls or muslin in your chosen perfume, and then wrap them round the soap. Seal the soap in a plastic bag and leave it for 2 months.

Scented Lingerie

To make scented drawer-liners, first place the given amount of oils for any perfume recipe on a cotton ball. Cut pieces of wall paper to fit your drawers, and rub the backs of them with the cotton ball.

You can also mix 4 tablespoons dried unscented flower petals with the oils of your choice. Do this by putting the petals into a plastic bag and adding 3 or 4 drops of your favorite oils. Seal the bag tightly and leave it for at least 2 days to allow the oils to soak into the petals. Then transfer the fragrant petals to a muslin bag and place it in your drawer.

Scented Notepaper

Using the method described above, mix 4 tablespoons of dried unscented flower petals with the oils of your choice. Place the muslin bag full of fragrant petals in your box of notepaper, and leave it for four weeks.

Fragrances for Confidence

The oils used in these pages will bring you courage, confidence and enthusiasm. Wear them when you are feeling warm, happy and self-confident, and also when you need an added boost, perhaps to give you courage at an interview, or when you are meeting someone for the first time. Not only will they help you to be yourself and feel good about it, they will also stimulate other people to realize that you are both confident and competent.

They are all quite bold scents, which indicate a self-possessed, outgoing personality in the wearer.

Inner Strength

I am the master of my fate,
I am the captain of my soul.

W. E. HENLEY,
Invictus

*To every 2 teaspoons
base, add the
following oils:*

4 DROPS LAVENDER
~
3 DROPS OAKMOSS
~
3 DROPS VIOLET
~
2 DROPS CORIANDER

The scent of violets is very clear, sweet, and somehow honest and, although it has no proven therapeutic use, it can remind you of younger days when life was uncomplicated. Violets were said to be the Empress Josephine's favorite flower, and Queen Victoria often wore a posy of fresh violets picked for her by Prince Albert. Used alone, the scent is too simple, but it is well complemented by the earthiness of oakmoss and the spiciness of coriander.

Refreshing lavender has calming properties and is also reputed to increase gentleness in men while giving greater strength to women.

Self Esteem

No coward soul is mine,

No trembler in the world's storm-troubled sphere....

EMILY BRONTË,
Last Lines

To every 2 teaspoons
base, add the
following oils:

4 DROPS YLANG YLANG

~

3 DROPS NEROLI

~

3 DROPS OAKMOSS

~

3 DROPS ROSEWOOD

Ylang ylang is at once rich, floral, and spicy and has a warming, sensual effect that helps to boost your confidence. Neroli is a stress-reducing oil that adds to the sweetness of the perfume. Oakmoss and rosewood complement the florals.

Oakmoss has a wonderfully rich, earthy quality, as well as the useful ability to act as a fixative in any perfume in which it is used. Rosewood is distilled from the wood chippings of a tree grown in South America, and its scent of roses and wood with a hint of spice is both warming and calming.

Awakening

We live in deeds, not years; in thoughts, not breaths;
In feelings, not in figures on a dial.
We should count time by heart-throbs....

P. J. BAILEY,
Festus

*To every 2 teaspoons
base, add the
following oils:*

4 DROPS LEMON
~
4 DROPS GRAPEFRUIT
~
2 DROPS YLANG YLANG
~
1 DROP CEDARWOOD

Grapefruit and lemon are refreshing and uplifting scents. Grapefruit oil can help you define your goals more clearly – when material goals become meaningless, it's time to sit down and work out what you really want from life. Both grapefruit oil and lemon can help you sort out new priorities.

The other-worldly fragrance of ylang ylang suggests hitherto unexplored possibilities, while cedarwood acts as a firm base both for the perfume, and for your emotions. Cedarwood is often used as a fixative in natural perfumes and has a soothing, harmonizing effect on the senses.

This perfume can help you to look at things in a new light and give you a sense of purpose.

Courage

Life is mostly froth and bubble,
Two things stand like stone,
Kindness in another's trouble,
Courage in your own.

ADAM LINDSAY GORDON,
Ye Wearie Wayfarer

To every 2 teaspoons
base, add the
following oils:

5 DROPS BERGAMOT
~
3 DROPS SANDALWOOD
~
2 DROPS JASMINE
~
1 DROP GRAPEFRUIT

Bergamot is distilled from the rind of the Bergamot orange and its warm, pungent scent can have an uplifting effect on the emotions, banishing self-doubt.

Sandalwood can also promote a relaxed confidence and its woody tones complement the floral sweetness of jasmine, which can help to give you the courage to face events optimistically. The Emperor Napoleon favored a perfume of Spanish jasmine, but whether he wore it to give himself courage, or for the seductive properties of its scent, we can only speculate.

These three oils, combined with a touch of grapefruit whose sharp citrus quality can be inspiring, will give you the courage, perseverance and optimism that you need to pursue your aims.

Decisiveness

White shall not neutralize the black, nor good
Compensate bad in man, absolve him so:
Life's business being just the terrible choice.

ROBERT BROWNING,
The Ring and the Book

To every 2 teaspoons base, add the following oils:

3 DROPS GRAPEFRUIT
~
3 DROPS BERGAMOT
~
4 DROPS NEROLI
~
3 DROPS CYPRESS

The scent of grapefruit oil can help you achieve the clear thought that is vital for decision making. Besides a sharp, citrus quality, its scent has much more – a warm, rounded pungency with hints of dryness and spiciness. Bergamot oil has similar qualities of fragrance, and has a warm and balancing effect on the emotions.

Neroli provides the sweetness, and its soothing qualities are said to reduce anxiety.

Cypress has a stimulating yet soothing aroma which suggests the inner confidence that welcomes the challenge of decision-making.

Calm Confidence

Wear your worries like a loose garment.

ANON

To every 2 teaspoons base, add the following oils:

4 DROPS JASMINE
~
1 DROP PATCHOULI
~
4 DROPS LEMON

Jasmine, the "King of flower oils," possesses many special qualities. In the ancient Egypt of the Pharaohs, only the privileged few were able to wear such a perfume. Now, although it is "rare" compared with other oils, and therefore more expensive, this exquisite oil is available to all, and fortunately a little goes a long way. Here, it has the power to inspire strength and confidence, calming and uplifting at the same time.

Sweet, musky patchouli eases stress and banishes any feelings of apprehension, and lemon cuts through the two richer scents with its special type of relaxing freshness.

Self Assurance

...to thine own self be true,

And it must follow as the night the day,

Thou canst not then be false to any man.

WILLIAM SHAKESPEARE,
Hamlet, Prince of Denmark

*To every 2 teaspoons
base, add the
following oils:*

5 DROPS YLANG YLANG

4 DROPS ROSE

3 DROPS LIME

2 DROPS CINNAMON

You know your style and you are confident that it works for you. You can admire other people without feeling jealous or overpowered.

The name ylang ylang means "flower of flowers." This starry-flowered plant that is grown in the Far East blossoms all year round, but the best oils are produced in May and June. It is widely regarded as a confidence booster, and its rich floral scent is both warming and soothing.

Rose brings a gentle touch, warm cinnamon gives that reviving touch of spice, and mellow citrusy lime adds an essential touch of freshness.

Wearing this combination of spice and citrus will help you to face the day confidently.

Panache

Something of old forgotten queens
Lurks in the lithe abandon of your walk.

GWENDOLYN BENNET,
To a Dark Girl

To every 2 teaspoons
base, add the
following oils:

**5 DROPS SWEET
ORANGE**

~

4 DROPS BERGAMOT

~

2 DROPS BASIL

~

1 DROP CORIANDER

This is an individual, stylish fragrance, which will enable you to sail through the day with style and verve.

Both basil and bergamot can banish shyness and self-doubt, and give you renewed faith in your abilities. Basil has a spicy quality to its scent which blends in well with the spicy freshness of coriander. Pure, stimulating bergamot adds a sunny note, and sweet orange oil softens and mellows the effect.

Fragrances for Relaxation

The fragrances in this section are designed
to establish inner feelings of tranquility
and security. The oils included in these
recipes have recognized properties for
relaxation, and you will find that very
quickly you come to associate their
scents with a clear, steady, and
calm state of mind. From time to time,
you need to focus on your inner, private
world – to re-center yourself after the
hurly-burly of external events which
constantly call on your quick, instinctive
responses. These fragrances for relaxation
will allow you to keep a clear head, but
will also encourage poise and serenity.

Stillness

There is a poem at the heart of things.

WALLACE STEVENS

To every 2 teaspoons base, add the following oils:

2 DROPS LAVENDER

~

4 DROPS NEROLI

~

2 DROPS SPEARMINT

Neroli is another name for orange blossom. It has a rich, warm, floral scent and in the sixteenth and seventeenth centuries it was often used for scenting gloves. It can help to ease anxiety and tension and give you a feeling of well-being.

Lavender has always been one of England's favorite scents, used both for pleasure and for its calming effects. Lavender perfumes and waters have been used to calm many an old-fashioned lady smitten with a hysterical attack of the "vapors," and sprigs of lavender were once sewn into nightcaps to relieve nervous headaches.

The stillness that you achieve with this scent can stay with you even when you become busy again.

Meditation

To see the world in a grain of sand
And a heaven in a wild flower,
Hold infinity in the palm of your hand
And eternity in an hour.

WILLIAM BLAKE,
Auguries of Innocence

To every 2 teaspoons
base, add the
following oils:

4 DROPS SANDALWOOD
~
3 DROPS LEMON VERBENA
~
4 DROPS MUSK
~
2 DROPS FRANKINCENSE

Regular meditation can refresh you both spiritually and physically and help you find the key to your being.

Frankincense has been used as an aid to worship and meditation in many different religions and beliefs for thousands of years. Its dry, woody scent helps you to regulate your breathing into a slower pattern and concentrate your mind. Sandalwood, when used in this fragrance, adds a woody sweetness. It can also help you to relax and feel secure. Zesty lemon verbena is another calming fragrance, and the musk is used purely for its rich, heady scent.

Harmony

Such harmony is in immortal souls.

WILLIAM SHAKESPEARE,
The Merchant of Venice

To every 2 teaspoons
base, add the
following oils:

2 DROPS YLANG YLANG

2 DROPS BERGAMOT

1 DROP CLOVE

1 DROP VANILLA

Ylang ylang is known to calm feelings of anger and frustration. Its rich, floral, and slightly spicy fragrance is balanced here by the refreshing citrus scent of bergamot, whose uplifting properties can induce self-confidence. The strong spiciness of clove and the richness of vanilla round off a well-balanced perfume.

Vanilla was first brought to Europe from South America by the Spaniards. The physician at the court of King Philip pronounced it "that smell of musk and balsam from New Spain." It has, however, no known therapeutic properties.

34

Contentment

All's right with the world!

ROBERT BROWNING,
Pippa's Song

*To every 2 teaspoons
base, add the
following oils:*

5 DROPS NEROLI
~
3 DROPS ROSE
~
1 DROP BASIL
~
1 DROP LIME

Think of sitting in a walled garden in the sun. Blossom is hanging over the wall, there are tubs of decorative oranges and pots of pungent herbs. You are relaxed and happy and life seems sweet – that is the atmosphere that is conjured up by this perfume.

The sweetness of neroli and rose are balanced by the refreshing scent of lime, and the herbal qualities of basil. In Elizabethan England, pots of basil were given by country women as gifts to visitors. A century later, John Gerard wrote: "The smell of basil is good for the heart and for the head, that the seede cureth the infirmities of the heart, taketh away sorrowfulness which cometh of melancholy, and maketh a man merry and glad."

Memories

Come to me in the silence of the night;

Come in the speaking silence of a dream;

Come with soft rounded cheeks and eyes as bright

As sunlight on a stream....

CHRISTINA ROSSETTI,
Echo

To every 2 teaspoons base, add the following oils:

3 DROPS JASMINE

~

2 DROPS ORANGE

~

1 DROP SANDALWOOD

A bundle of love letters tied up with ribbon lying forgotten at the bottom of a drawer, a diary recording the rapture of a first love, or an old photograph.... This combination of scents has a nostalgic, slightly wistful mood.

The evocative sweetness of jasmine allows you to distance yourself from the hectic nature of everyday life and take a peaceful saunter down memory lane. The rejuvenating properties of orange give you the strength not to regret, but to look back with pleasure at the happy times, achievements, and important milestones in your life, and not to dwell on anything negative. Lastly, there is sandalwood, to help you relax and be at peace with yourself.

Relaxation

Life is painting a picture, not doing a sum.

OLIVER WENDELL HOLMES JR,
Speeches

To every 2 teaspoons base, add the following oils:

6 DROPS SANDALWOOD
~
4 DROPS ORANGE
~
2 DROPS ROSE
~
1 DROP PINE
~
1 DROP LEMON

Sandalwood is a powerful scent whose woody sweetness enables the wearer to break free from the day's pressures.

Orange is the most mellow of the citrus oils. Sweet and rich with a hint of sharpness, its delicate warmth can relieve any remaining tension.

Rose oil is calming and emotionally healing and its sweet perfume has been popular through the ages. It was a great favorite with Marie Antoinette, who had a special rose and violet scent made up for her by the perfumier Houbigant.

These sweet scents are offset by the sharper aromas of pine and lemon, which offer their own relaxing freshness.

Fragrances for Vitality

The fragrances here will help to bring the sweet, fresh breath of country air into your life, to make you feel like soaking up the sunshine, shaking your hair in the wind and running free.

The oils they contain are mainly the florals and herbals that remind you of flower gardens, herbs in pots and country meadows. Overall, they are relaxing, refreshing, and uplifting.

Some will also help you to concentrate your thoughts and help you be more aware of your inner self and the world around you.

Escape

The heart of a woman goes forth with the dawn,
As a lone bird, soft winging, so restlessly on,
Afar o'er life's turrets and vales does it roam
In the wake of those echoes the heart calls home.

GEORGIA JOHNSON,
The Heart of a Woman

*To every 2 teaspoons
base, add the
following oils:*

6 DROPS YLANG YLANG
~
3 DROPS CLARY SAGE
~
2 DROPS LEMON
~
1 DROP LAVENDER

Ylang ylang oil can soothe away anger and stress, relax your mind and lift your emotions. It has a deliciously sweet, floral scent that needs the herbal qualities of lavender and clary sage, and the freshness of lemon to lighten its exotic qualities and bring it back to earth.

Clary sage is the happiness herb, with an ability to lift the dullest of moods. If it is used just before you go to bed it will help you to sleep, but may also bring about vivid dreams. Some people who have tried it in an air freshener in their working environment have found it *too* euphoric – there are some times when you should not try to escape!

In Touch

What is this life if, full of care,
We have no time to stand and stare.

W. H. DAVIS,
Leisure

To every 2 teaspoons
base, add the
following oils:

6 DROPS ROSE
~
5 DROPS BASIL
~
3 DROPS MANDARIN
~
2 DROPS CEDARWOOD

There are times when your awareness is heightened and you can see things much more clearly, or they appear in a new light. This added perception can be physical or mental.

Basil can clear your head and give your mind strength and clarity, revive you, and make you feel mentally alert. The "speakers" or wise men of the Fang tribes of Africa used to chew basil leaves in order to gain inspiration and assurance while taking part in the native ceremonies known as "palavers."

Rose softens and smooths the basil's herbal scent, while mandarin provides a sweet freshness. Cedarwood is regarded as a harmonizing oil and provides a pleasantly woody base.

Country Girl

FLORAL AND CITRUS WITH A HINT OF SPICE

*They were gathering flowers, roses and crocuses and
beautiful violets in a soft meadow.*

ANCIENT GREEK trs. JULES CASHFORD,
Hymn to Demeter

*To every 2 teaspoons
base, add the
following oils:*

6 DROPS JASMINE
~
4 DROPS LIME
~
1 DROP CLOVE

Although jasmine is native to Asia and India, it has long
been grown in gardens in England, America, and
Europe. Its scent is rich, warm and floral, and a sniff of
jasmine in the middle of a hectic day is a lovely way to give
yourself a refreshing memory of a Mediterranean vacation
by the sea. Although jasmine is relaxing, it is also uplifting,
and can inspire confidence and optimism.

Like all the citrus oils, lime has a refreshing quality which
can conjure up the fresh country air.

Clove oil is an age-old remedy for toothache and is
still sold by pharmacists for its analgesic properties.
Here it is used simply for its spicy sweetness.

Charm

*If you have charm, you don't need to have anything else;
and if you don't have it, it doesn't much matter what
else you have.*

J. M. BARRIE,
What Every Woman Knows

*To every 2 teaspoons
base, add the
following oils:*

2 DROPS LAVENDER

2 DROPS ORANGE

2 DROPS CINNAMON

1 DROP CLOVE

Lavender, so redolent of an English country garden, is the most "charming" scent there is. It is fresh, sweetly floral, and its refreshing and relaxing qualities are a constant reminder of gentle country simplicity and old fashioned virtues. It was the favorite perfume of Nell Gwynne, whom Charles II certainly found extremely charming. At their secret meetings he followed the custom of the time and gave her presents of sachets of dried lavender.

This delightful perfume combines lavender with the citrus scent of oranges, and the warm, spicy sweetness of cinnamon and clove.

Vitality

The same stream of life that runs through my veins night and day runs through the world and dances in rhythmic measures.

RABINDRANATH TAGORE,
Gitanjali

To every 2 teaspoons
base, add the
following oils:

6 DROPS CARNATION

~

2 DROPS LEMON VERBENA

~

1 DROP CLARY SAGE

~

3 DROPS SANDALWOOD

You feel wide-awake, fresh and ready to go. You have boundless, inexhaustible energy that keeps you going from early until late.

In ancient Greece, carnations were highly prized. Their name *dianthus* comes from the Greek *dios*, meaning Zeus or God, and *anthos*, meaning flower – literally, "flower of God." Carnation oil has a sweet and spicy scent that is often associated with health and energy, and can also be an aid to concentration.

Clary sage adds a whiff of euphoria to this mixture and lemon verbena gives a feeling of release from stress. This refreshing, zesty mixture is warmed by sandalwood.

Enthusiasm

Nothing great was ever achieved without enthusiasm.

RALPH WALDO EMERSON,
Essays

*To every 2 teaspoons
base, add the
following oils:*

5 DROPS LEMON

~

4 DROPS GRAPEFRUIT

~

2 DROPS MANDARIN

~

5 DROPS YLANG YLANG

The tanginess of lemon can stimulate the senses, adding vitality to your efforts, whether at work or play. Grapefruit and mandarin have similar citrus qualities which are both refreshing and uplifting.

The zestful nature of these citrus oils is offset by the intense floral sweetness of ylang ylang. It is one of the few oils which can stand on its own as a perfume, and is also used as a fixative for other oils. Its ability to stabilize the emotions will help you to target your energies and keep your boundless enthusiasm in check.

Free and Easy

FRESH AND SWEET WITH SPICY UNDERTONES

Go home and put my man out
If he don't treat me right,
Wild women don't worry,
Wild women don't have the blues.

IDA COX,
Wild Woman Blues

To every 2 teaspoons
base, add the
following oils:

4 DROPS JASMINE
~
2 DROPS LEMON
~
1 DROP BERGAMOT

You're happy and free and have the day to yourself to do as you please. Relax, let go and enjoy yourself, and do what suits the moment. This perfume has a light quality which will match your mood.

Here, jasmine is used for its relaxing properties. Its delicious floral scent does wonders for your emotions, lifting them free of habitual worries and concerns.

Lemon is tangy and refreshing, ensuring that the perfume suits your light-heartedness, but stimulating your senses to enjoy your freedom to the utmost.

Laughter

*There's nothing worth the wear of winning, but laughter
and the love of friends.*

HILARE BELLOC,
Dedicatory Ode

*To every 2 teaspoons
base, add the
following oils:*

3 DROPS JASMINE

**3 DROPS
SANDALWOOD**

Sometimes you have to laugh. Not at anything in particular. It's just a feeling, a happy impulse inside bubbling
up until you have to let it go. This combination of oils, rich,
but not too sweet, is both exciting and stimulating: very
appropriate for this delightful feeling.

Jasmine's luxuriant floral perfume is a powerful anti-
depressant, indicating renewed optimism and well-being.

Sandalwood's rich tones can promote both physical and
mental well-being. It is traditionally associated with self-
expression, not being afraid to show – and share – your
high spirits by laughing aloud.

Fragrances for Happiness

Perfume plays a subtle, but vital part in
setting a scene and creating a mood, and
the fragrances in this section are perfect for
when you're feeling light-hearted; when
you've woken up feeling that problems are
insignificant, that the world is your oyster,
and that really, anything is possible; or
when you're down and in need of
a pick-me-up. There is a range of
fragrances to suit a rainbow of moods:
exuberance, good-humor, flirtation,
romance, and the sheer joy of being alive
on a beautiful day.

Joyfulness

On with the dance! Let joy be unconfined;
No sleep till morn, when youth and pleasures meet
To chase the glowing hours with flying feet.

BYRON,
Childe Harold's Pilgrimage

To every 2 teaspoons
base, add the
following oils:

2 DROPS CLARY SAGE

2 DROPS CARNATION

4 DROPS MANDARIN

3 DROPS JUNIPER

To conjure up joyfulness, that expansive feeling of life having endless possibilities, try blending this perfume.

Clary sage is the herb of happiness and elation. It can lift dull spirits when you are low, or intensify the feeling of well-being when life is going well. Its dry, herbal scent, with a faint hint of sweetness, is well complemented by the carnation which is sweet with a hint of dryness.

The refreshing fragrance of mandarin oil and the dry spiciness of juniper balance the more euphoric qualities of the clary sage and help you capture, and hold, that feeling of light-hearted joy.

Cupid's Arrow

I think I will go to my love
And tell to him my mind.

TRADITIONAL FOLK SONG,
Bushes and Briars

*To every 2 teaspoons
base, add the
following oils:*

2 DROPS GRAPEFRUIT

1 DROP SANDALWOOD

3 DROPS JASMINE

1 DROP CINNAMON

Your mind is made up, and it's time to do something about it. You're going to declare yourself, to propose, or perhaps to accept. This bold scent is the perfect perfume for such an occasion.

Sandalwood gives its warming qualities to this rich perfume, helping to keep you happily relaxed, and aiding self-expression. It was very popular with Elizabeth I, herself a bold woman, who used it to scent her linens and clothes.

Jasmine is here again, with its intensely feminine seductive qualities. Grapefruit oil is added to help you make the right decision, to keep you emotionally strong, and to establish clarity of thought. It also lightens this otherwise heady mixture. Add a touch of spicy cinnamon, and the whole combination is one of love with a purpose.

Lovers' Meeting

SWEET AND FLORAL WITH A HERBAL UNDERTONE

Has not the rose, since history began, spoken of love, hiding the fragrant mystery under velvet petals of most gentle hue?

ANNA LEA MERRITT

To every 2 teaspoons base, add the following oils:

4 DROPS ROSE

~

2 DROPS JASMINE

~

1 DROP BERGAMOT

This perfume contains jasmine for joy and passion, and bergamot for confidence, but its main scent is of roses.

Rose oil, long associated with love and romance, was first discovered in India when Jehangir, the Mogul emperor, murdered the husband of the Princess Nourdjuhan Beygum, "the sun among women," and married her himself. At their wedding he had the canal in the imperial gardens filled with rose petals. While walking beside the canal, the bridal pair noticed a fragrant oil that had floated to the top and they ordered it to be collected. The princess named it after her lover, A'ther Jehangiri.

Cleopatra, who adored rose petals, had her floors strewn with them, scattered them on her bed, and even stuffed her pillow with them to welcome Antony.

First Love

I ne'er was struck before that hour
With love so sudden and so sweet,
Her face it bloomed like a sweet flower
And stole my heart away complete.

JOHN CLARE,
First Love

To every 2 teaspoons base, add the following oils:

5 DROPS NEROLI
~
3 DROPS JASMINE
~
2 DROPS LIME

When you are in love for the first time and that love is returned, you have a wonderful glow about you which affects everyone you meet.

The scent of neroli is as sweet and delicate as a first love. It is named after a princess of Nerola in Italy with whom it was a great favorite. She wore it as a perfume all the time, poured it into her bath and used it to scent her gloves.

Jasmine adds richness and a hint of passion, and lime gives a tangy lightness of heart. All combine to make the warm, exciting scent of first love.

53

Sweet Tease

Maybe yes, and maybe no,
You may have it as you please.

D. H. LAWRENCE,
Tease

*To every 2 teaspoons
base, add the
following oils:*

3 DROPS GRAPEFRUIT
~
3 DROPS LEMON
~
2 DROPS SPEARMINT
~
1 DROP BERGAMOT

Perhaps you don't want him after all.... Or perhaps you do. Maybe you've changed your mind. Will you or won't you?

While you think about it, lemon keeps you relaxed while the dry spiciness of bergamot underscores your playful mood. Spearmint soothes any ripples you may cause. The sharp, citrusy quality of grapefruit will help you decide – eventually. There's no hurry, you're feeling light-hearted and flirtatious, and you're both enjoying the game, so why rush into anything? You've got it all to look forward to, and after all, traveling hopefully can be just as much fun as arriving.

Flirtation

My cheeks you have with blushes filled,
My heart with fits of laughter.

ANON

*To every 2 teaspoons
base, add the
following oils:*

5 DROPS ORANGE
~
3 DROPS JASMINE
~
3 DROPS SANDALWOOD
~
2 DROPS PATCHOULI

The first jasmine to grow in Europe was from a cutting that was planted in the garden of the Duke of Tuscany in Italy. When the tree had grown sturdy, legend has it that the head gardener took a cutting and gave it to a lady on whom he had had his eye. She grew it so successfully, and made so much money from the perfumes that she made from the distilled flowers, that she married him in gratitude, and carried a bouquet of jasmine at her wedding. Although it is basically floral, jasmine has underlying tones of warmth and richness.

The powerful scent of patchouli can soothe away any stress and its earthy scent deepens the overall perfume. It was one of the essential ingredients used in Guerlain's exciting perfume Shalimar.

Happiness

My heart is like a singing bird.

CHRISTINA ROSSETTI,
A Birthday

*To every 2 teaspoons
base, add the
following oils:*

5 DROPS ROSE
~
4 DROPS LEMON
~
3 DROPS BERGAMOT
~
2 DROPS CINNAMON

This fragrance is pure happiness — warm, outgoing, and generous. The rose, so loved by many women and frequently incorporated into expensive perfumes, gives its own special sweetness and gentle warmth. The relaxing freshness of lemon makes your senses more receptive and spicy cinnamon gives a warm glow. Bergamot's ability to lift your spirits will make your happiness complete.

Bergamot was one of the original ingredients of eau-de-Cologne, possibly the most successful commercial scent ever invented. It was first made by an Italian, Giovanni Maria Farina, in 1725. Bergamot's own scent is a combination of warm, round pungency and sharp, dry spiciness.

Warmth

A great ring of pure and endless light
Dazzles the darkness in my heart.

MADELEINE L'ENGLE,
A Ring of Endless Light

To every 2 teaspoons
base, add the
following oils:

2 DROPS SANDALWOOD

1 DROP JASMINE

1 DROP ROSE

1 DROP BERGAMOT

You may not be jumping for joy and clapping people on the back, but a gentle feeling of inner warmth makes you feel at peace with the world and radiate contentment.

The scents in this perfume all have a warm quality. The rich scent of sandalwood encourages a feeling of easy relaxation. This is enhanced by the floral sweetness of jasmine and rose which help to keep at bay anxiety, tension, and emotional problems.

Bergamot's uplifting properties can also invoke a feeling of inner warmth while its hint of sharp, dry spiciness prevents this perfume from being too rich and cloying in its sweetness.

Fragrances for Love and Luxury

The fragrances in this section are two-fold.
Some are for the times when you feel the
need to pamper yourself, revel in
luxurious self-indulgence, and emerge
feeling glamorous and ready for a
great night out. Other scents are
essentially warm and seductive, perfect
for adding an exciting, honeymoon feel
to a romantic evening. They can be as
rich and earthy as you like, with a strong,
almost savage appeal – or elegant and
sophisticated, if the mood takes
you that way.

Passion

You will be my lover
And I shall be your Queen.

SHIONA PHILIPS,
Samhain

*To every 2 teaspoons
base, add the
following oils:*

7 DROPS SANDALWOOD
~
2 DROPS ORANGE

This seemingly simple mixture of sandalwood and orange combines to make a deep, rich perfume. Sandalwood is ideal if you want a perfume to last all night, and its warm pungence gives out a powerfully sensual scent.

Sandalwood is traditionally associated with security, joy, self-expression, and relaxation – everything that a good relationship should bring. Its scent is rich and warm, with a woody sophistication.

Orange oil is the most mellow of the citrus oils. Its delicate sweetness spells an end to tension, and its rejuvenating properties will make you feel eternally young. Together, these two oils will make you feel deeply relaxed and very seductive.

Sophistication

… the general air, the style, the self-possession.

LOUISA M. ALCOTT,
Good Wives

To every 2 teaspoons base, add the following oils:

3 DROPS LINDEN BLOSSOM

2 DROPS ORANGE

1 DROP CYPRESS

1 DROP NEROLI

There are times when you need to be confident, cool, and slightly detached from the rest of the world. The luxurious, unusual fragrance of linden blossom will enable you to wear your mood like a designer suit, and a dash of dry, astringent cypress can help to give you the strength and inner assurance to carry it off with style. If you are not able to obtain linden blossom, the distinctive scent of rose geranium makes a good alternative.

Orange provides sweetness with a sophisticated twist, while neroli, one of the essential ingredients in any good eau-de-Cologne, will give you that cool, confident feeling.

Ecstasy

POWERFUL, SWEET, AND WOODY, LIGHTENED WITH A TOUCH OF MINT

If that same golden moon were overhead
Or if beneath our feet, we did not know.

ELIZABETH BARRETT BROWNING,
Aurora Leigh

To every 2 teaspoons
base, add the
following oils:

3 DROPS JASMINE
~
1 DROP SPEARMINT
~
1 DROP GINGER
~
1 DROP SANDALWOOD

This is the perfume that simply says "sex." Use it when you are sure of a passionate encounter.

Here, jasmine is used for its sensual, luxuriant perfume, which is expressive of joy and passion. Rich sandalwood is also known for its sensual properties, and its exotic, warm scent is ideal for evening wear as it will last all night – you'll even wake up smelling wonderful in the morning.

Even unbridled passion must have a little control, and refreshing spearmint will allow you to catch your breath.

Warm spicy ginger enhances physical energy and promotes sexual arousal, and it has long been used for these purposes in South-East Asia where it was first discovered, many centuries ago.

Seduction

A RICH MIXTURE OF FLOWERS AND WARM CITRUS

I would go with you to my orchard.
I would go with you to my garden.
There I would plant the sweet, honey-covered seed.

Poem celebrating the marriage of the goddess Inanna

*To every 2 teaspoons
base, add the
following oils:*

7 DROPS JASMINE
~
3 DROPS ORANGE

Seduction is all about creating the right mood, something Cleopatra knew very well when she had the sails of her barges drenched in aromatic oils so that she could waft up the Nile to Antony on a fragrant breeze. Before synthetic perfumes were produced, all perfuming was done with essential oils and unguents, but not always with the intention of setting the scene for an enchanted evening. Sometimes it was to mask other, less pleasant smells.

Jasmine is one of the oils like rose, patchouli, sandalwood, and ylang ylang, whose heavier aromas are well suited to the bedroom, so they're right for wearing at times when you're feeling sexy. Jasmine's rich floral scent is complemented here by the citrus warmth of relaxing orange.

Exotique

A cargo of ivory,

And apes and peacocks

Sandalwood, cedarwood and sweet white wine.

JOHN MASEFIELD,
Cargoes

To every 2 teaspoons base, add the following oils:

8 DROPS GARDENIA

~

3 DROPS VANILLA

~

3 DROPS ROSEWOOD

~

3 DROPS ROSE

It is said that one of the finest traditional scents is a combination of rose, "white flowers," and vanilla, and this is very similar to it.

Sweet gardenias have always been regarded as a luxury flower. They can bring that inner peace without which the outside would never look so great. Vanilla is seductive and inspires physical energy, while rosewood brings alertness and keeps you going on a late night date. The rose is quietly seductive, but at the same time relaxing.

This is a combination to make you dazzle in front of the bright lights.

Woman

She moves a goddess, and she looks a queen.

ALEXANDER POPE,
Homer's Iliad

*To every 2 teaspoons
base, add the
following oils:*

8 DROPS MUSK
~
4 DROPS SANDALWOOD
~
3 DROPS OAKMOSS
~
2 DROPS PATCHOULI

Musk, sandalwood, oakmoss, and patchouli are an earthy and sensuous mixture that is unashamedly female. This mixture forms the base of the perfume sold to complement *La Perla*, Italy's range of luxury lingerie.

The musk oil that is now readily available is a synthetic oil, not the original one, which was of animal origin. It does not, therefore, have any great aromatherapy value, but its heady, evocative scent is still wonderful. It was the favorite perfume of Napoleon's Empress, Josephine, who perfumed her boudoir with musk, and it is said that the scent lingered in the room for years after her death.

Luxury

... days of wine and roses

ERNEST DOWSON,
Vitae Summa Brevis

*To every 2 teaspoons
base, add the
following oils:*

6 DROPS GARDENIA
~
3 DROPS NEROLI
~
4 DROPS SANDALWOOD
~
2 DROPS OAKMOSS

This perfume is an ideal complement to a bath full of warm bubbles, a basket of fruit, and your favorite champagne on ice.

Sandalwood brings relaxation and warmth. At the court of Akbar in Ancient India, sandalwood was combined with orris root, aloes and a special lichen to create an incense called Chavela. The Arabs had a similar substance and called it Rushafza. The lichen, which was said to grow on oak and cypress trees but is unknown today, was probably similar to oakmoss which has a rich and earthy scent. Neroli simply adds to the feeling of luxury.

The sweet scent of gardenias will help you to unwind, relax, and pamper yourself.

Velvet

...O so soft! O so sweet is she!

BEN JONSON,
The Underwood

*To every 2 teaspoons
base, add the
following oils:*

8 DROPS NEROLI

8 DROPS SANDALWOOD

2 DROPS LIME

1 DROP CORIANDER

Neroli has the ability to calm any nervous apprehension and increase relaxation and enjoyment. It was once put into bridal wreaths and bouquets to induce these feelings in the bride and groom.

In the Middle East and Europe, coriander has been valued as a love potion and aphrodisiac. In *The Arabian Nights*, it was one of the ingredients in the love potion prepared by the hashish seller in the story of Ala-al-Din Abu-al. His concoction included frankincense and honey, but here, coriander is blended with refreshing, tangy lime, warm sandalwood, and neroli, to make a lush, mellow perfume.

Notes

The preceding recipes should get you started on mixing scents at home, but you will quickly find out which oils most appeal to you, and you should adapt the suggested proportions to suit your own taste. Just one drop more or less can make all the difference in creating a scent that is uniquely yours.

It is easy to lose track of the exact number of drops you have added when making the recipes, however, so use these pages to take notes as follows.

SCENT

OILS   TOTAL DROPS

COMMENTS

SCENT

OILS   TOTAL DROPS

COMMENTS

SCENT

OILS   TOTAL DROPS

COMMENTS

SCENT _____

OILS _____ TOTAL DROPS
_____
_____
_____
_____
_____

COMMENTS _____
_____
_____
_____

SCENT _____

OILS _____ TOTAL DROPS
_____
_____
_____
_____
_____

COMMENTS _____
_____
_____
_____

SCENT _____

OILS _____ TOTAL DROPS
_____
_____
_____
_____
_____

COMMENTS _____
_____
_____
_____

SCENT _____

OILS _____ TOTAL DROPS
_____
_____
_____
_____
_____

COMMENTS _____
_____
_____
_____

SCENT _____

OILS _____ TOTAL DROPS

_____

_____

_____

_____

COMMENTS _____

_____

_____

_____

SCENT _____

OILS _____ TOTAL DROPS

_____

_____

_____

_____

COMMENTS _____

_____

_____

_____

SCENT _____

OILS _____ TOTAL DROPS

_____

_____

_____

_____

COMMENTS _____

_____

_____

_____

SCENT _____

OILS _____ TOTAL DROPS

_____

_____

_____

_____

COMMENTS _____

_____

_____

_____

Directory of Suppliers

Advanced Health Foods
679 Anderson Avenue
Cliffside Park, NJ 07010
(201) 946-7582

Angelica's Herbs
147 First Avenue
New York, NY 10003
(212) 529-4335

Aphrodisia
264 Bleecker Street
New York, NY 10014
(212) 989-6440

Aroma Vera
5901 Rodeo Road
Los Angeles, CA 90016
(310) 280-0407

Aveda
509 Madison Avenue
New York, NY 10022
(212) 832-2416

Belle Star, Inc.
23151 Alcalde, #C4
Laguna Hills, CA 92653
(800) 442-7827

The Body Shop by Mail
45 Horsehill Road
Cedar Knolls, NJ 07927
(800) 541-2535
The Body Shop is

located in:
Arizona/California/
Colorado/Connecticut/
Florida/Georgia/Illinois/
Kansas/Louisiana/
Maryland/Massachusetts/
Maine/Michigan/
Minnesota/Missouri/
New Hampshire/New
Jersey/New York/North
Carolina/Ohio/Oregon/
Pennsylvania/Texas/
Virginia/Washington/
Washington D.C./
Wisconsin

Bodyography
1023A Third Avenue
New York, NY 10021
(212) 421-6650
and
**Century City Shopping
Center**
10250 Santa Monica
Boulevard
Los Angeles, CA 90067
(310) 552-4660
To order, call
1-800-642-BODY

**Caswell-Massey
Company**
111 Eighth Avenue
New York, NY 10011
(800) 326-0500

Cherchez
Front Street
Millbrook, NY 12545
(914) 677-8271

Common Scents
3920A 24th Street
San Francisco, CA 94114
(415) 826-1019

The Essential Oil Co.
P.O. Box 206
Lake Oswego, OR 97034
(503) 697-5992
and
3638 S.E. Hawthorne
Boulevard
Portland, OR 97214
(503) 236-7976
and
710 N.W. 23rd Avenue
Portland, OR 97210
(503) 248-9748

Kiehl's Pharmacy
109 Third Avenue
New York, NY 10003
(212) 677-3171

Leydet Aromatics
P.O. Box 2354
Fair Oaks, CA 95628
(916) 965-7546

Madini Oils
68F Tinker Street
Woodstock, NY 12498
(914) 679-7647

Nature's Elements
Stores are located in:
Massachusetts/New
Hampshire/New Jersey/
New York/Pennsylvania
(800) 545-1325

**The Original Swiss
Aromatics**
P.O. Box 6842
San Rafael, CA 94903
(415) 459-3998

Palmetto
1034 Montana Avenue
Santa Monica, CA 90403
(310) 395-6687

Ra-Bob International
6646 S. 143rd Street East
Derby, KS 67037
(316) 776-9556

The Soap Opera Inc.
30 Rockefeller Plaza
Concourse 16
New York, NY 10112-0001
(212) 245-5090

Uncommon Scents, Inc.
380 W. First Avenue
Eugene, OR 97401
(503) 345-0952

Index